D1234034

I See Orange

Trudy Micco

Bailey Books
an imprint of
Enslow Publishers, Inc.
40 Industrial Road
Box 398
Berkeley Heights, NJ 07922
USA
http://www.enslow.com

Bailey Books, an imprint of Enslow Publishers, Inc.

Library of Congress Cataloging-in-Publication Data

Micco, Trudy.
I see orange / Trudy Micco.
p. cm. — (All about colors)
Summary: "Learn about the color orange"— Provided by publisher.
    Includes bibliographical references and index.
ISBN 978-0-7660-3791-5
1. Orange (Color)—Juvenile literature. 2. Color—Juvenile literature. I. Title.
QC495.5.M475 2011
535.6—dc22
                                        2010011883

Paperback ISBN: 978-1-59845-166-5

Printed in the United States of America

062010 Lake Book Manufacturing, Inc., Melrose Park, IL

10 9 8 7 6 5 4 3 2 1

Photo Credits: Shutterstock.com

Cover Photo: Shutterstock.com

Note to Parents and Teachers

Help pre-readers get a jumpstart on reading. These lively stories introduce simple concepts with repetition of words and short simple sentences. Photos and illustrations fill the pages with color and effectively enhance the text. Free Educator Guides are available for this series at www.enslow.com. Search for the *All About Colors* series name.

Contents

Words to Know 3

Story 5

Read More. 24

Web Sites 24

Index 24

Words to Know

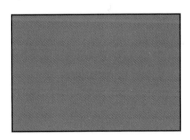

orange

oranges

I like orange.

I like orange.

7

I like orange.

I like orange.

I like orange.

I like orange.

15

I like orange.

I like orange.

I like orange.

21

I like orange oranges.

Read More

Gordon, Sharon. *Orange.* Tarrytown, N.Y.: Marshall Cavendish Benchmark, 2008.

Jones, Christiane C. *Autumn Orange.* Minneapolis, Minn.: Picture Window Books, 2007.

Web Sites

Enchanted Learning. *I Love Colors: Shades of Orange.* <http://www.enchantedlearning.com/colors/orange.shtml>

Do2Learn. *Colors.* <http://www.dotolearn.com/games/whatcolor/pages/index.html>

Index

like, 5, 7, 9, 11, 13, 15, 17, 19, 21, 23
orange, 5, 7, 9, 11, 13, 15, 17, 19, 21, 23
oranges, 23

Guided Reading Level: **B**
Guided Reading Leveling System is based on the guidelines recommended by Fountas and Pinnell.

Word Count: 31